The Poems of Junior Clark

Edited by Mel Clark

THE POEMS OF JUNIOR CLARK

First edition. February 23, 2022.

Copyright © 2022 Mel Clark.

ISBN: 979-8201744632

Written by Mel Clark.

Table of Contents

<u>Preface</u>

My uncle, Junior Clark wrote when he had something to say. I don't know when he started. From reading through his work, I'd guess his earliest poem was written when he was in his late fifties or early sixties.

His topics are varied. The common theme is his own strong feelings. He wrote about things that mattered to him, Family, People, Places, Nature, God.

Some of his pieces move me to tears.

They are all Junior's words. I just assembled them in this volume. I hope you enjoy them as much I as did.

Regards,

Mel Clark,

November 4th 2021

Acknowledgements

Junior wrote the poems. Putting them together was a labor of love. But I couldn't have done it by myself. Junior and Ella's daughter, Teri Gale Mundy, found the various poems. She provided them to me along with some family photographs.

Junior's sister Betty (Penny) Aaron and her daughter Kristi also helped and provided encouragement.

Thanks to all of you.

Thanks also to the love of my life, my wife Linda. She tolerates my writing habit and sometimes she even encourages it. I love you, Linda.

<u>Introduction</u>

Welcome to this volume of poems penned by Junior Lee Clark. We hope, that by venturing into these, you will have a snapshot of the man he was.

Junior Lee Clark was born on October 12, 1927. In his lifetime he saw and participated in a lot of history. He grew up during the Greta Depression and the economic hardships following until the beginning of WWII.

Junior joined the US Navy and served abord the battleship USS Missouri. The Missouri was where the Japanese Emperor Hirohito signed the "Instrument of Surrender", effectively ending the War in the Pacific.

Returning home after the war, he set about starting a career and a family. He and his wife, Ella, produced two children. Their son, Jerry, was eldest, followed by a daughter they named Terry.

Junior Lee Clark was a man of many interests. He stayed engaged and active in the business and enjoyment of life until his final and fairly rapid decline.

Among his interests were genealogy. Spending many hours looking through records at the historic Fincastle Courthouse in Virginia's Botetourt County, he traced his ancestors back as far as possible.

His other interests included history, hunting, all things outdoors, woodworking, and of course, his family.

To really know a man, you must first learn what he loved. The loves of his life were his family, his church, and his God.

Junior was always there for his family. He enjoyed his children and the children they produced as time went by. He didn't just watch, he participated. He coached girls' softball when his grand daughters Layci and Kyndall played. He looked forward to hunting with grandsons Landon and Seth Cullen. He made himself available, understanding that spending his time with them was the greatest gift he could give them.

He supported his wife in her interests, going to flea markets, yard sales, shopping, church activities, beach vacations, and other activities they could share.

Junior Lee Clark loved his country. Exemplified by his military service. He was an unabashed supporter and enthusiastic cheerleader and supporter of this land. It grieved him to see many of the issues that brought unrest to the country he served. He was unapologetic in his support and love for the US.

Junior Lee Clark also loved his God. He was a faithful member of his church, serving on the Board of Deacons. His leadership in that role was gentle, never seeking the spotlight. He dedicated himself to supporting the church in all its functions.

Finally, and the point of this book, is the fact that Junior Clark was a rustic poet. He was NOT a hillbilly poet, but he couched his phrases in plain fashion.

I was once asked to type a work of his, and being me, I set about making certain changes. He gently took me to the woodshed, pointing out that he had said EXACTLY what he intended in the way he intended to say it. I learned from that woodshed experience to not impose myself between an artist and their intended purpose. He knew what he wanted to accomplish; I did not.

So, here we are. Welcome to the works of Junior Lee Clark, expressed as he wished.

These poems are not grouped in any particular order but are simply offered for your pleasure. It's our hope you will come away from the experience with a sense of the man; his wit, his humor, and his style.

Please enjoy the ride.

JUN   59

My Home Town

There is a place I love to be, most dear to my heart,
Nestled in the foothills of the Upper James, the little town of Eagle
Rock.
It's been said there was a mighty eagle that used to fly,
Where the river meets the mountain and the mountain meets the sky.
Once the river was bustling with bateaux carrying iron ore,
The mines ran out long ago and the bateaux float no more.
Sometimes when I'm dreaming of another day and time,
Old memories come creeping from the shadows of my mind
Of a barefoot lad, a mom and dad,
A fishing pole, a swimming hole, and the best friends I ever had.
The Eagle broke its wing in the flood of eighty-five,
We lost most everything; we barely did survive.
Once the streets were busy and happy voices soared,
Now the streets are empty and the stores have closed their doors.
We can't return to yesterday, and the way it was back then,
But I long to see it come back long enough
For the wing to heal,
And the Eagle to soar again.

Junior Lee Clark
2013

Railroad Ave

Southern Roots Hair Salon
Eagle Rock Lime Kilns
Eagle Rock
Eagle Rock Baptist Church
James River

The Old Swimming Hole

When I was a young lad, many years ago
The most favored place in all the world that I loved to go
With all my friends and my fishing pole
Was down by the river to the old swimming hole.
We would swim and play as long as there was light
Then we'd build a bonfire, fish & tell ghost stories 'way into the night.
Growing up in the Great Depression times were hard and things were
bad
But when you're a kid you don't miss what you never had.
One Sunday morning we heard someone on the radio say
That something bad had happened in a land far away.
A place we had never heard of before,
A place called Pearl Harbor; we were going to war.
On that fateful Sunday evening, little did we know
That before it was all over many of us would have to go.
One by one we were called by Uncle Sam
To go and serve our country in a far and distant land.
By the grace of God, we all survived;
I was thankful that we came back alive.
We would still get together every now and then
We'd talk about the things we did and the places we had been.
We would listen to all the stories we were told
But we never made it back to the old swimming hole.
Things had changed; they could never be like they were back then.
We left home as boys and came back as men.
Sometimes my memory takes me back to my childhood long ago.
I think of all the things we did and the old friends I used to know.
It makes me sad, and yet I feel so richly blessed
All my old friends have passed on and I'm the only one that's left.
If God would grant me one last request

Before He takes me home to my eternal rest
When He asked me what I had in mind,
I'd ask Him to take me back to 1939.
To a warm summer day, a barefoot lad with his fishing pole
With all my old friends, down to the river, to the old swimming hole.
Junior Clark

8-27-14

High S
745
2nd St
Church St
688
43
Eagle Rock United
Methodist Church
James River
James River

A Four Wheel Lady-Tracking Machine

Two good old boys out to fulfill a dream
In a four wheel lady-tracking machine.
A gas miser to the last drop,
It was a little red jeep with a silver top.
That little jeep was a young man's dream
I'm not sure if it was a chick magnet
Or a four wheel tracking machine.
Wouldn't it be good to go back in time
And see those old friends of yours and mine.
Now we are two old friends riding off into the setting sun
With a treasure of memories of the things we have done
That was a different time and a different place.
But old memories cannot be erased,
Of two young boys growing up in Eagle Rock
And that little red jeep with a silver top.

The Ghost of Thunder Mountain

By Junior Clark

It was the coldest opening day I could remember. The temperature was 14 degrees, the wind was blowing 15-20 miles per hour, it had snowed four days prior, turned warmer and melted into a slush. It turned bitter cold, turning the mountain into an ice cap and the trees looked like giant icicles making it impossible to hunt.

I took my stand near one of the many paths leading to the bedding grounds. I was in search of the ghost, or phantom as he was sometimes referred to. This was not an ordinary buck. Some folks say he weights 400 pounds and had twenty points. Some say he was even bigger. I had seen him a few times but he had never given me a good look, just a glimpse and he was gone. All I knew was that he was the biggest buck I had ever seen. All the hunter in the valley wanted to claim bragging rights for bringing in the ghost, but he always seemed to bring out the worst in them.

It was 6:30 a.m. a half hour before daybreak. 6:30 turned into 7:30 then 8:30. My fingers felt like icicles. I wondered if I could pull the trigger if I got the chance. I thought about the warm fire, hot coffee, and biscuits and gravy that awaited me at home. But nothing could take my mind off of this unforgiving wind. 9:30 then 10:30. I could hear a crush crush in the ice. It seemed to be coming straight at me.

At 50 yards it stopped. I could see the outline of a very large deer. He turned his head to look back. I could see one side of his antler. No doubt that this was the phantom. I raised my 303 British and set the iron sights on his brisket. Not a good shot but I had to take what he gave me for he would be gone in a few seconds.

I squeezed the trigger and heard a loud click, as if you had stepped on a dry stick on a still night. He wheeled and ran back in the direction from which he had come. Later that day I learned that the firing pin had frozen. The rest of the season I looked for a sign of the ghost, but he had vanished living up to his name.

That spring I was in the village when something caught my eye in the window of a local hardware store. It was a shiny new Winchester with a telescope sight. If only I could afford that rifle, things might be different. Every time I went to the village, I found myself in front of the window. Once I had to buy some hardware, the store owner was busy with another customer, and again I found myself looking at that rifle. When the store keeper was finished, he walked over to where I stood admiring that rifle.

He said he had noticed me looking at that rifle for quite sometime and wondered if I was interested in purchasing it. I explained how I would love to own a gun like that but could not afford it. I thought to myself how it would take forever to pay for and what I would have to give up in order to do so, but it would be worth it if I could bah that buck up on Thunder Mountain. I had him work out the monthly payments and took it home. I could hardly wait until the season started.

When September came, I was on the mountain looking for signs. From September to November not a trace of the Phantom could be found. Where could he be> The whole state would know if he were to be killed. The next year brought the same luck ... He was no where to be found. September of the following year I was again on the mountain looking for a sign. When I got to the place where I had seen him three years earlier, there was a scrape as big as a barn door with tracks as big as a yearling steer. A white pine with a rub four feet high. No mistake, he was back. Excitement was running high, and although I knew it was a mock scrape, I knew he would be back. When the rut started two months later, I picked out a spot about sixty yards from the scrape, under a white pine with the branches touching the ground. There I would build my blind.

I was careful not to move much brush at a time. He would notice anything unusual, a little at a time. By November it was finished. Now all I had to do was wait. On opening day I was in the blind before dawn. I waited till dusk and he did not come. The following day ... the same. One thing I had learned, it takes patience to fool an old buck. All that week I waited and he never came. On Tuesday of the second week around four p.m. I saw the form of a large deer in the shadows coming to the scrape.

Cautiously he approached the scrape and then stopped. I had never seen such a beautiful animal. He looked every bit of four hundred pounds. His horn was wide as a man's hand. I counted nine tires on either side. They looked to be sixteen inches high, and his dark brown coat seemed to glitter.

I raised my rifle and set the cross hair on the white spot on his neck. For the next few seconds a hundred thoughts must have raced through my mind. I remember every time I had ever seen him, all the years I had hunted him. I remembered the day in the ice storm three years prior. With one squeeze of the trigger, it would all be history. He's become a legend I though, a monarch. He is as much a part of this mountain as the trees and the rocks. He belongs here. Somehow the bragging rights seemed unimportant to me. I lowered my rifle. From now on I would spend as much time protecting him as I had trying to take him. Now he was looking straight at me. For a moment it seemed our eyes were welded together. Just then I felt a bond of friendship between that buck and me. He never spooked and ran as he always did. He nodded his head and looked back. Then he as if he understood. He walked ten paces, stopped and looked back. Then he returned slowly into the forest. He is still up there on the mountain and I guess he always will be. Sometimes he disappears for months at a time ... but he always returns. Some still call him the phantom, most folks call him the ghost of Thunder Mountain, and some even call him Ol' Chocolate.

My Old Home Place

By: Junior Clark.
I looked upon my old home place, the place where I was born,
The window sash was broken and the curtain old and tom.
The place was cold and empty, with no one living there,
The porch was sagged and breaking down in bad need of repair.
The only sound that I could hear was the chirping of a bird
Where once so many years ago, my mother's voice was heard.
I looked upon the yard where once flowers grew and happy voices
soared.
Now the fence had rotted down and the flowers grew no more.
Now the family is growing old and gone their separate ways.
I'm in the twilight of my yeans and numbered by the days.
Jesus promised in the Bible, "I go to prepare a place for you,
In my Father's house, beyond the starry blue,"
I don't want a mansion made of gold and fancy lace,
I just want a house up there just like my old home place

ONLY HALF WAY THERE

At a birthday party of this friend of mine,
He swore he was only thirty-nine.
But, if the truth was ever told,
This man's a half a century old.
He was born in the days of F.D.R.
The model A Ford and the trolley car.
King George sat upon the throne,
And ice cream was still a nickel a cone.
He got addicted to chicken when he was 3 years old,
Or at least, that's the way the story is told.
His dad used to look at him and say,
This boy will grow up to be a preacher someday.
He can grab a chicken leg as quick as a cat,
Nobody but a preacher can eat chicken like that.
The boy would just look at his dad and grin,
And wipe the gravy from his chin.
He'd take another bite or two,
And eat the whole chicken before he was through.
He grew up to be a strong young man,
And became the best preacher in all the land.
He preached the love of God with every word,
He was the best preacher we ever heard.
He'd spread the gospel wherever he'd go,
I guess that's why we love him so.
Now he's getting older and slowed down a might,
But he's still got a powerful appetite.
A lot of chickens have lost their heads,
Just to keep this preacher fed.
He's got a bad back and a busted knee,
He has to have glasses now before he can see.

He's had eight operations and he's loosing his hair,
But if he lives to be a hundred,
HE'S ONLY HALF WAY THERE!

Written By: Junior Clark
    For: Wessley's Surprise Birthday Party
    Date: July 12, 1987
    Place: E.R. Firehouse

A Christmas Story

I stopped at a country store one day to buy some gas for my jeep. There was an old man sitting there in a rocking chair with a dog laying at his feet.

I paid for my gas and started to leave, the
old man said mister if you have a few minutes to spare I'll tell you a story you'll find hard to believe.

I said I'm in a hurry I'll sit for a while and he leaned back in his rocker with a great big smile.

He said I had a friend once who had a dog he called old Fuz, he was the best bear dog there ever was.

He did have one fault I'll have to admit when old Fuz took a track he never quit.

I was hunting one day with this friend of mine I think it was in the year of 89.

When a voice came over the old CB it said head up boys this is Gene and me.

We just jumped a big one up here on the Honts Peak, he's heading straight off the mountain to Mill Creek.

I thought to myself how lucky can one man be, the way those hounds are running they're coming straight at me.

I ran up on the ridge as fast as I could, I unzipped my coat and threw back my hood.

He's so close now I can hear him run, I pushed off the safety and shouldered my gun.

When he came in sight there went all my luck them hounds were chasing an 8 point buck.

Old Fuz was leading the pack then Bonzo and old Black Jack,
then all Gene's dogs made up the rest of the pack.

Fire seemed to fly from old Fuz's teeth, he was nipping and biting at that big buck's feet.

All at once that buck took a mighty lunge toward the sky and started running above the tree tops about 30 feet high.

I could be wrong I suppose but I saw a red light on the end of his nose.

He turned on that little red light, headed north and faded out of sight.

Now I never believed in Santa Clause and I'll tell you why. I never believed that reindeer could fly,
but if you could have been with me that day you'd see how those May's dogs made a believer out of me.

They lost Fuz that day he never came home. John said a bear may have got him up there on the mountain all alone,
or maybe he just ran so far that day that he got lost and couldn't find his way.

Last Christmas Eve I heard a strange sound, I ran outside and looked all around.

Right there before my very eyes was old Santa Clause and his reindeer streaking through the sky.

Old Rudolf was out front shinning his light to guide old Santa through the dark foggy night

and then I heard an old familiar bark of a hound, there is only one dog in the world that could make that sound.

There he was plain as day that black fuzzy dog was chasing the sleigh.

I told you before he had one bad fault I'd have to

admit when old Fuz takes a track he just won't quit.

I thanked the old man for his story, walked

back to my jeep and put on my hat. I thought to myself there's nobody but a bear hunter that could tell a tale like that.

JOY

ODE TO THE BEAR HUNTER

I've been following these hounds for nye on to a week,
   I've got a bad cold and can hardly speak.
   My coat's getting ragged and my shoes are thin,
   But I feel awfully good for the shape I'm in.
   The game warden's threatening to write me up,
   For not having a tag on my red bone pup,
   My back is so sore it will hardly bend,
   But I feel awfully good for the shape I'm in.
   I've got arthritis in both my knees,
   And when I talk, I talk with a wheeze,
   My pulse is weak and my blood is thin,
   But I feel awfully good for the shape I'm in.
   When the season is over and the bear is denned up,
   And I'm sitting by the fire with my coffee cup,
   It is better to say I'm fine with a grin,

Than to let people know the shape I'm in.
Junior Clark

MOTHER BY JUNIOR CLARK

IT'S BEEN SO LONG SINCE MY MOTHER PASSED AWAY.

I MISS HER AND THINK ABOUT HER NEARLY EVERY DAY.

I MISS HER SMILE AND THE KIND WORDS SHE USED TO SAY.

BUT WHEN I MISS HER MOST IS ON MOTHER'S DAY.

WE WOULD GATHER AROUND THE TABLE ON THAT HER SPECIAL DAY.

I CAN CLOSE MY EYES AND HEAR HER NOW AS SHE BOWS HER HEAD TO PRAY.

I KNOW SHE'S UP THERE IN HEAVEN AND I'LL SEE HER AGAIN SOME DAY.

FOR NOW I'LL SAY "I LOVE YOU MOM, AND HAPPY MOTHER'S DAY."

IF YOU STILL HAVE YOUR MOTHER, TELL HER YOU LOVE HER AND KISS HER SOFTLY ON THE FACE.

FOR THERE IS NO OTHER IN ALL THE WORLD CAN EVER TAKE HER PLACE.

TIME GOES BY SO SWIFTLY AND SOON THERE WILL COME A DAY,
THE HANDS OF TIME WILL CATCH UP TO HER
AND SHE TO WILL PASS AWAY.
CALL HER OFTEN AND WHISPER SOFTLY THOSE THREE WORDS SHE WOULD LOVE TO HEAR YOU SAY.
I LOVE YOU MOM, HAPPY MOTHER'S DAY.

The Game We Almost Didn't Win

The outlook was grim for the Lady Knights that day,
    The score was four to two with one inning left to play.
    When Burrell grounded out at first and Ramsey did the same,
    A sad sickness came upon the home fans at the game.
    Some got up to leave in deep despair, but for the rest,
    A spark of hope loomed eternal in their breast.
    They thought if only Layci could get a whack at that,
    She had two RBIs the last time at the bat.
    But Kelly Thompson preceded Layci, as did Heather Bartee.
    Thompson had struck out twice and Heather was 0 for 3.
    So when the crowd considered that,
    It seemed but little chance of Layci getting to the bat.

But Thompson let drive a single to the wonder of it all,
And Bartee hit a long drive off the left field wall.
When the dust was lifted and they saw what had occurred,
Bartee was safe at second and Thompson was at third.
Then from the stands, there went up a might roar,
Like angry storm waves beating on a far and distant shore'
It echoed from Purgatory Mountain to the Cherry Bottom Flat,
For Layci, number 10 was advancing to the bat.
There was ease in Layci's manner as she stepped into place,
There was pride in her bearing as she dug in at the plate.
Five hundred eyes were on her as the rubbed her hands in dirt,
Five hundred hands applauded when she wiped them on her shirt.
While the left-handed pitcher ground the ball into her hip,
Assurance gleamed in Layci's eyes, a sneer was on her lip'
Now the pitcher winds and throws and Layci ducks her head,
"That's too high" said Layci," "strike one!" the umpire said'
"Kill him, kill the umpire" someone shouted from the stand,
And it's likely they'd have killed him had not Layci raised her hand.
Again the pitcher winds and throws and again the ball flew,
'"That's too low" said Layci, the umpire said" Strike two!"
"Fraud!" cried the fans, and the echo answered "Fraud!"
Layci raised her hand, called for time and the angry crowd was
stalled.
Through her Christian charity, her sportsmanship was shown,
She calmed the angry crowd and bade the game go on.
They saw her face grow stern and cold, the saw her muscles strain,
And knew that Layci wouldn't let the ball go by again'
The sneer was gone from Layci's lip, her teeth were clinched in hate.
She pounded with cruel violence, her bat upon the plate.
The pitcher held the ball, and then she let it go,
And then the air was shattered by the force of Layci's blow.
The crowd was on their feet, then came a mighty roar,

The ball had cleared the fence by thirty feet or more!
As she ran the bases, she trotted into fame,
The score was five to four, the Knights had won the game!
Where the Knights will go from here, only time will tell,
But Layci had her job to do, and she did it well!

ODE TO THE CAMPER

by
Junior Clark

In this great land of ours
    Where mountains meet the sky,
    Where trucks roll down the highway
    Now and then a camper goes by.
    They're heading off to somewhere
    With excitement in their heart,
    If there's good times to be had
    You can bet they'll have their part.
    They come from all walks of life
    Some are even called to preach,
    One thing they have in common
    Come summer, they'll all be at Myrtle Beach.
    They're honest hard working people
    But yet they are proud,
    Just look and you can see them

They stand out in any crowd.
If you're in need anywhere
Across this great big land,
There will always be a camper there
To lend a helping hand.
So hats off to all the campers
From North, South, East, or West,
You always have and always will
Be among America's best.
When their life on earth is over
And time for them will be no more.
When they cross that silent river
And reach that distant shore,
Saint Peter will be there to greet them
And he'll take them by the hand
He'll say, "Come with me my children,
Today you'll be camping in Canaan Land."
"I know you campers love the beach
So come and follow me,
I'll put you with your old friends
Over by the Crystal Sea."
"No, you don't have to bring your trailer
It's getting worn and old,
We're giving you a new one
That's made of solid gold."
If you've ever pulled a camper
Down a long highway,
Or walked the sandy beaches,
On a warm summer day
Or waded barefoot
In a cool mountain stream
You know that's life at its fullest

And that's the camper's dream.
So here's to all the campers
I mean it when I say,
It's guys and gals like you
That make America great
The way it is today!

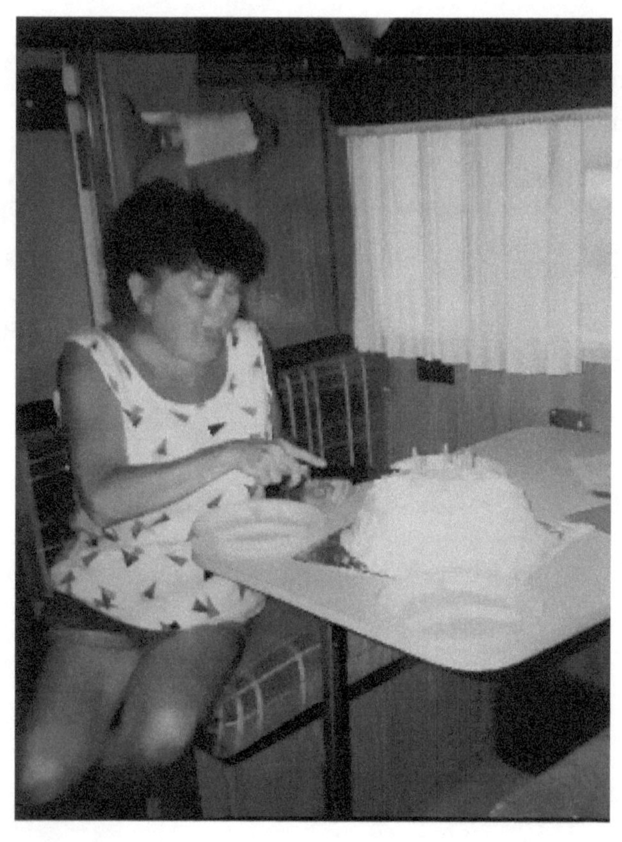

THE MAN WHO CHEATED HIMSELF

There once was a man, a carpenter by trade.
Who took great pride in the things that he made.
He could build you a house,
Or make you a chair.
Everything he made he did with great care.
He worked hard all his life,
But could not get ahead.
He barely kept his family fed.
And when he could save a few pennies each day,
It seemed there was always another bill to pay.
In this town, there lived a rich man
With much money and land.
Who had compassion on the poor unfortunate man.
He said to the carpenter one day with a smile,
I'd like you to come work for me awhile.
I want you to build me a house on three acres of ground.
On that vacant lot at the edge of town.
Built it 40 by 60 and 30 feet tall,
With three baths and plush carpet from wall to wall.
With a large sun porch and a big swimming pool
Where the children can play when they come home from school.
Use only skilled labor, and the very best material you can find.
I want this house to be the only one of its kind.
I'm going on a long journey. When I return again,
I'd like the house ready to move in.
This made the carpenter so happy as he thought with a smile
At least now I will have a job that will last for a while.
He was thinking that night, as he lay in bed,

This may be my one chance to get ahead.
If I hire cheaper labor and use cheaper material instead,
For once in my life, I might get ahead.
In a few days, he started to build,
With his unskilled labor and his cheaper material.
If a board was sawed crooked and didn't fit,
He would just fill it with putty and paint over it.
Soon people were coming from miles around
to see this new house at the edge of town.
It was a beautiful house to see.
But beneath all that putty and paint,
The carpenter knew, it wasn't what it ought to be.
Such a beautiful structure, so cozy and warm.
But he wondered could it ever weather a storm.
When the rich man returned from his journey he found,
this beautiful house at the edge of town.
The carpenter said to him, come I want you to see
The house I built for you, here is the key.
The rich man said, I have admired your work for years,
And I have watched you toil through the sweat and tears.
And to me, it just didn't seem right,
That I have so much, and you go to bed hungry, night after night.
I wanted to do something to help you, you see
That house you built is yours, you keep the key.
The carpenter was so ashamed that he wanted to run,
As he thought of that awful thing he had done.
While trying to cheat the rich man out of part of his wealth,
In the end, he wound up cheating himself.

The Road of Life

When I asked you if you'd be my wife,

And travel with me down the highway of life,

I knew there would be mountains to climb and rivers to cross both deep and wide.

But I knew we could make it with you be my side.

There would be road blocks and detours and bridges to burn.

Down the Highway of life there is no return.

We endured the tunnel of hardship and financial strain.

But not once did I hear you complain.

Then the road seemed to get smoother day after day.

And we raised two children along the way.

I thank you my darling for being my wife.
And traveling with me down the highway of life.
It's been a good journey we've had a good ride.
We conquered the mountains and rivers so wide.
Somewhere up ahead when we grow old,
We'll reach the highway that's paved with gold.
To the highway of life, we'll say goodbye,
And take the Heavenly expressway that leads to the sky.
JR

TRIBUTE TO A LADY

Of all the great ladies the world has ever known

There is one among us today that stands alone.

Always thinking of other in her own unique way

This special lady turns fifty today.

Devoted to her church and dedicated to God

She seems to walk where the saints have trod.

She's been through a lot of suffering and pain

But not once have we heard this lady complain.

So considerate of others as everyone knows

She brings a little sunshine wherever she goes.

When we count our blessings, we're so thankful we met

This special lady we call Jeannette.

She has so much love for others, she's so willing to share

Even though she has her own burdens to bear.

Someone like her comes along only once in one's life

This special lady – our pastor's wife.

July 14, 1991

Junior Clark

The Unfaithful Servant

When God created the universe, He set America apart,
Far from Europe and Israel, the Holy Land, the jewel of His heart.
He put America here for a reason, that no one can deny,
A guardian over Israel, the apple of His eye.
Now prayer has been taken from the classroom, the Ten
Commandments from the wall.
How long will God let this go on, before He lets America fall?
Your greed for lust to stay in power has let our country down.
Someday you will have to answer when you hear that trumpet sound.
When the roll is called up yonder and time on Earth will be no more,
And you find yourself locked out on the wrong side of the door.
And the book of life is opened and your name can not be found,
Ask yourself this question, "Was the going up worth the going down?"
You are an unfaithful servant, you're a cheater and a liar.
Now you must spend eternity in the lake of fire.

J. L. Clark

2013

QSIVE
TIT NI
RT

Karen

When I was a young man of two
score and nine,
A little girl came to live
next door, who would soon
be a favorite niece of mine.
I watched her growing up,
She was such a happy child.
She was always so well mannered,
And wore a friendly smile.
Now that you are all grown up,
You turn thirty-four today,
You know we've always loved you
In a very special way.
I know that you will always be
that favorite niece of mine.

September '91
Junior Clark

A Whisper in the Wind

Once I saw a mountain, it was so beautiful to see.
  As I gazed upon its beauty, it seemed to beckon me.
  When I climbed its rugged slopes and reached the summit there,
  The view it offered me was far beyond compare.
  Thirty miles to the north the purple mountains glow,
  The farm lands and winding river I could see far below.
  Overhead a red-tailed hawk sored on his morning flight,
  To me this was a most breathtaking sight.
  A breeze began to blow, and I heard a voice in the wind,
  "I'll share with you my secrets, if you will be my friend.
  Many men come to my forest, but none will be my friend,
  They cut my trees and kill my game and they are gone again.
  I want someone who will come back often, on whom I can depend.
  I have much to offer you if you will be my friend.
  I will always be here for you as long as you shall live,
  Take only what I offer you, not more than I can give."
  Then all was still, I heard not another word.
  Was this my imagination or was it a voice I heard?
  The words kept going through my mind, though I could not comprehend
  One thing I knew for certain – I must go back again.
  When next I gazed upon her splendor, I heard the voice again,
  "I was hoping you'd return – welcome back my friend."
  When I walk through her forest, I never feel alone,
  For my mountain friend has become my second home.
  Many years have come and passed since I heard the whisper in the wind,
  Through all those silent years, she's been my faithful friend.
  Sometimes when I feel lonesome and an true friend can't be found,

I go back to the mountain, up to that hallowed ground.
When I stand on its highest peak where few mortal men have trod,
I feel so close to heaven, I can almost touch the face of God.
When my life is almost over and I can see the setting sun,
Just over the horizon I will hear the distant drum.
I know my spirit will dwell forever on this mountain that I love
While I keep a watchful eye from my cabin up above.
On some autumn morning, if you listen close my friend,
I'll share her secrets with you as I whisper through the wind.
And if by chance you should love this old mountain as I do,
Take good care of her my friend, and she'll take care of you.
By Junior Clark

About the Editor

This photo was taken in 1999. Mel Clark (second from the right) is one of Junior Clark's (on the far right) nephews. Mel and Linda (center) live in Lynchburg, VA about 50 miles East of Junior's hometown of Eagle Rock, VA. Junior's wife, Ella, is second form the left. Their granddaughter, Kendal, is at the far left.

Mel has written a number of books, mostly about personal finance, retirement planning, and the martial art of Neko Ryu Goshin Jitsu. His books can be found at

https://books2read.com/ap/xXk1N8/Mel-Clark

or using the QR Code below.